To the joys of life: Ocean, sun, sand, mountains, laughter, coffee aroma, rain and earth smell.

To our favorite consumers and business, and marketing students.

To our students of literature and fiction

To our kids, friends, and family members

Hail to the King of Sneakers: Michael Jordan Nike Air Jordan Retro Time

(A social media-loaded, marketing campaign, success story)

Hail to the King of Sneakers: Michael Jordan's Nike Air Jordan Retro Time (A social media-loaded, marketing campaign success story)

King of the Hill: The Jordan Brand's Athletic Footwear, Apparel..

Kevin Levin

Nike Inc. promotes safety and security among shoppers caught in a frenzy over the sale of its sneakers. Once upon a time, I was also stung by the collector's bee that's in each one of us. Here are two of my favorite pairs of Nike Air Jordan Sneakers. I always feel comfortable wearing them.

These and other pictures of The Jordan Brand or Nike Brand sneakers or any other shoes <u>are not a display of these items for sale.</u> They are only part of the fictionalized marketing campaign and story of <u>this eBook.</u> As a result, if you purchase this eBook, <u>you will not obtain a pair of shoes with its download or print format.</u>

Table of Content:

placements, marijuana smoking just to create an edge and facilitate the purchase of a few pairs of sneakers

8. Fathers and mothers to abandon their kids and brace the natural elements

9. Signs of the time: The Battle of Brands, Team Nike Air Jordan vs. Team Adidas

10. Word of mouth, word on the Main Street, and buzz marketing principles

11. Word of mouth, fads, buzz in the times of social media such as Twitter, G+, Pinterest, Facebook, Instagram, and the growing power of WhatsApp, YouTube, Streaming Videos, Netflix etc.

12. Transforming the desires for a product into a frenzied sale

13. Brawls, slaps, take-downs, pepper spray sessions, stampedes, and riots are the immediate results of effective and efficient word of mouth, social media, and buzz marketing campaigns

14. The Jordan Brand: Sneakers, Athletic Footwear, Apparel, and Gear

15. Building a shoe empire: Superstar, Hero, Businessman Michael Jordan speaks up, 'Democrats and Republicans wear shoes.'

Chapter 1
Taking New Flight With
Nike Air Jordan XI Concord

Two days before Christmas or even much earlier these days, the buying power of most American shoppers gets revived. The shopping season has just begun. And for those who are the members of Amazon Prime, the shopping season may have begun way earlier, sometime in June or July depending on the company's schedule. In fact, most American shoppers usually start amassing presents for the next holiday season right after Christmas and the new year. In general, shoppers are going from stores to stores looking for the 'It' product. For sure, the latter has not been presented to the anxiously waiting mass of consumers. The malls and retail store managers were still waiting for a miracle product to appear. They were waiting for the product that would cause their clients to literally break down their front door. They would like to see the crowd that waits nights and days, in good and bad weather, in front of the Apple stores. They may not want to see the brawls that take place at all the Wal-Mart stores.

Thanks to the analysis of their clients' buying history, they now know that American shoppers want to go retro, but not on any items. Thanks to great analytics and algorithm, they also know that the young shoppers could take the lead. They also know that they will never have enough of this hit product to sell to each one of their consumers. For weeks, the leaders of this top brand, (Michael Jordan, Jordan, Nike Jordan) and the retail industry have been working on the best ways to release their new products. The fans of the famed Chicago Bulls have been waiting too. They wanted to see the same miracles that Michael Jordan performed to their delight when the team won consecutive championships. The release of the magic product – for which shoppers are willing to suffer, cause injury, shoot to kill, get sent to jail or fight, receive a few doses of pepper spray discharge – could not come at such a better time. After all, they have been trying to go back down the memory lane. More importantly, these avid fans want a good reason to get out and camp in front of the malls and retail stores to purchase a few pairs of the top sneakers of their favorite players. The best of the 7 final games leading to the NBA championship or crowning of a winning team is also about the battle of the sneaker brands worn by top players. The brands sponsoring the specific players also go to the final games. The winning team is also the winning brand. In general, fans know what they want to their loved ones. They want to give a great holiday present to their sons and daughters, significant other, family members, husbands, boyfriends or partners.

Among all those varied groups of shoppers who come from all social or economic strata, we find the collectors who have appreciated these sneakers from the beginning. Nike started producting these shoes in the 1980s, especially in 1985. Many of these basketball fans converted themselves into collectors ready to spend thousands of dollars to purchase all the releases of the air Jordan sneakers. Way before the rest of the population found out what they were up to, these avid collectors saw a great business idea. As a result, they have become basketball fans – Air Jordan sneaker collectors – entertainers. This explains why a music star such as Kanye West getting deaply involved in sneakers. He sides with Adidas to release Yeezy Boost 350. Over the years, many of the fans get involved into this sneaker collection for bragging rights. And they can talk about Bulls' championship seasons with the same accuracy as they can regale you with the history of the shoes. For this specific group, Nike could expect to make a great business. Now it's worth saying that Nike's competitors are not sleeping. They also want to take a portion of the sweet pie. Adidas sets its goal in the future. It signs long-term contracts with major players and superstars in various sports. All the collectors could have bought the limited edition of sneakers released by Nike Inc.

Believe it or not, Nike Inc. counts on those collectors, superstars, top athletes of various sports disciplines as influencers and evangelists of the brand. Many sneaker fans are known to keep their shoes in their original boxes. They only take them out to wear on special occasions. They do not wear them on rainy days. Go to the house of any sneaker collectors. You will see that they dedicated a specially locked room to their collection. From the 'sapeurs' of Brazzaville and Congo to the urban lifestyle of America, you will encounter people who prefer to spend on their shoes, sneakers, than on their own needs. They have long chased their other family members' belongings out of their collection room. They did not get their way without a huge fight until the family members and they reached a working agreement. Such was the case of one of my best friends. He had to build his wife her own shoe room too.

To the right sneaker collectors, these shoes are as valued and worthy as gold. In many U.S. cities, Nike Jordan shoe owners have reportedly been mugged, shot at and even killed by thieves who want to make a quick cash. According to them, these sneakers are as precious as gold. For emotional reasons as well as good manufacturing, the Air Jordan brand has been a huge hit with bot sneaker collectors as well as non-collectors. For sure, for a long time, there have not been too many products that were able to rival or compete with this product. Nike Inc. must now continue to develop and improve if it wants to stay ahead. Adidas and other brands are coming up very strong. They want their piece of the pie. For many years, nostalgia and resale value of these shoes have caused many people to do anything they can to buy a few pairs.

Nike will no longer have to spend huge amount of money on advertising to recruit the true and diligent buyers of sneakers, the 10 to 20-year old group who is all too ready to skip school, work and other family engagements to be able to spend hours in front of stores. Nike Air Jordan has already established itself among this group. Now the 20+ fans and sneaker enthusiasts are also competing with the younger crowd for the same products. This confluence of factors, coupled with the fact that this company had a long history of releasing a limited amount of shoes may explain why so many consumers – young as well as old – want to lay their hands on a few pairs. In addition, these sneakers were selling like hot pies because Michael Jordan remained a very important personality in the sport and business world. He also managed to maintain his golf and business interests in check. In the past few years, an oversupply of Nike Air Jordan sneakers led to a reduction in sale quantity. Buyers did not see the need to rush out to buy a few pairs. At the same price, the costs were going up. That was also when the competitors found a niche to start nibbling Nike's business. And young people started feeling cool wearing Adidas again.

Yet, despite his retirement, Michael Jordan remains as popular as ever. Everyone who has ever stepped on a basketball court wants to be 'like Mike.' Which better way to show their enthusiasm other than to imitate his great ball moves, wear what he wears, and endorse the products that bears his trademark moves. Needless to say that on and off the court, Michael remains the consumate business man who has been able to create a winning template for the marriage of sports and commerce. Years later, superstar players such as Lebron James, Stepen Curry, Kevin Durant, Kobe Bryant will pay homage to Michael's savoir-faire. To his credit, Michael should be able to profit and take advantage of his acumen. It now makes sense that the products he designs or endorses still commend a large price and create chaos in the marketplace. Michael's business principles and acumen should be an open book for all athletes who have worked hard to secure a great contract paying them $ millions during their playing seasons. Many of them never think about how to keep the money coming during their retirement. Like Michael Jordan, they should think about long-term investments so that the money machine never stops.

If Steve Jobs was the brain and marketing pitchman for Apple, Michael Jordan is the uncontested pitchman and king of basketball. Many players of basketball will envy his good fortune. Others such as Lebron James, Stephen Curry, and Kevin Durant want to copy his moves on the court but also off the court. Kobe Bryant was rumored to have consulted with Michael Jordan on business, investments, and negotiation issues. For many reasons, a lot of fans baptized him as Michael's replacement. When it comes to the league, it has been a matter of taking a look at the players who can bring fans to the game. Kobe's explosion and success on the court were the subject of comparison in many aspects. Many reports showed that Michael did not hesitate to mentor him in the early days of the Lakers phenom. For sure, the list of athletes from multiple sports who want to imitate Michael Jordan is long. From football, tennis, soccer to basketball, we can find athletes who want to work on deals guaranteeing them to have a great work life after they leave their sports.

The genie has long been out of the bottle. With top security, Nike has been able to coordinate the shipping of millions of pairs of Air Jordan 11 Retro Concords to many malls and retail stores all over the country. Unlike a blockbuster movie release, bestseller book release, the release of Air Jordan 11 Retro Concord caused many people to have a huge headache. In view of the fights, frenzy, chaos, live brawls caused by the release of the sneakers, Nike had to issue a statement, "Consumer safety and security is of paramount importance. We encourage anyone wishing to purchase wishing to purchase our product to do so in a respectful and safe manner."

For sure, crowd control is a good, money-making problem for a company to have two days before Christmas. Shoppers were going nuts over its sneakers. They were pushing, breaking into lines, shoving each other, smoking pot to keep warm while they were completely exposed to the elements.

What companies such as Apple, Nike, Google, Microsoft and others have been able to capitalize on is the explosive power of power, of the perennial word of mouth or WOM and buzz in the times of social media. This is where Facebook, Twitter, Pinterest, G+, Instagram and others come in handy. They have become major players in connecting shoppers to products via the recommendations of friends, tweets, and circle. It did not take these companies a long time to realize that these new tools are just reincarnations of something they have known all along. With the right recommendations for their products, consumers will riot to get access to them. Setting the right price to sell them becomes secondary. It made sense that Nike and the Jordan Brand started being sold on a limited basis. That gave the buyers the idea that they were buying a luxurious product. But when the Nike and Jordan brand started being sold to the mass, there was a problem of oversupply. The competitors had an opportunity to market their products to the limited number of consumers who want not only to collect great sneakers but also buy the products at a price the ordinary Joes could not afford. How else can anybody explain the presence of these two parallel economies? One that has enough shoppers who will go to great lengths to get products such as iPhones, iPads,

Kindle Fires and more than $250 Nike Air Jordan sneakers and the other one that is frozen in time by unemployment, foreclosure, and job losses.

A multi-pronged, well-orchestrated campaign for the Nike Air Jordan XI Concord Sneakers resulted in the flooding of shoppers to the doors of retail stores and malls of the United States. Brawls, slaps, takedowns, pepper spray sessions, stampedes, and riots are the immediate results of effective and efficient word of mouth, GroupOn, social media, advertising, online ads, and buzz marketing campaigns. For sure, the sneaker collectors do not reside only in the United States of America. They are a special breed of consumers who can be found anywhere else in the world, especially the developping world where the economies can support such exclusivity and refinement of taste. They will shop for very specific sneaker brands irrelevant of the price hike. Yes, in this field, superlatives bordering dysfunctions do exist. From Japan, India, South Korea, France, England to China, the new Nike Air Jordan sneakers will continue to attract hordes of consumers.

For any marketer, transforming dreams into a sellable set of realities is a new high, a certain level of success that is incomparable. Up to Steve Jobs's death, the transformation of a high desire for Apple products had been the hallmark of his time as the top evangelist of the company. The same can be said for Nike which has avoided releasing its products on school days to avoid students' truancy and workers' lack of productivity or sickness calls from the malls or store counters. However, in the past few years, it's worth noting that these purchases can be done at any time on any day. Online stores have made it possible for shoppers to purchase their favorite products even while in the confession booth of most catholic churches or chapels. With the right innovative product targeted at the right group caught in a frenzy by the right marketing campaign highly influenced by the new social media, the mass of shoppers can only come rioting and stampeding to the malls of America and anywhere else in the world.

The preceding info partially deals with the background and the unveiling of the show we constantly watch or witness in the malls and retail stores of America. All it takes is for us to go shopping on any Thanksgiving day or the day after to witness the chaos and madness that exist because of top items that shoppers are attracted to. On YouTube and many other social media sites, one can sit in the comfort of his/her own home to follow the escalation deriving from limited sales.

Chapter 2
Two Days Before Christmas: Sneakers Agogo, Pushing and Shoving at Shoe Stores
'Tis the Season to be Jolly, La, La, La'

Think again if you sneakers were only shoes. The release of these Nike Retro Air Jordan basketball shoes was the cause of so much mayhem all over the country on December 23, 2011. From Richmond, CA, Stockton, Oakland, Santa Barbara, San Francisco to Georgia, Boston, Florida, New York, New Jersey, crowds of customers had been lining up. They wanted to purchase the new Jordan shoes. In places such as Richmond, store managers were afraid to open their doors. Most other inner cities where you will find shoe stores selling Nike Air Jordan shoes, store owners took additional security measures. However, those security guards could not walk with all the shoppers to their cars and their homes where thieves were expecting to rob or inflict much pain to get the shoes. It was a catch-22 for most store managers who were relying on high volume sales. Yet, they could not face those customers who were ready and willing to break their front doors down to buy those shoes. Customers were turned away from the Hilltop mall. A certain level of insecurity was briefly when a firearm was discharged. Police officers intervened to arrest a young man. Many shoppers got very upset over the store manager's decision. They had been waiting in line for what seemed to be an eternity.

"I am here because I want to own something that will last. And when I am tired of wearing the sneakers, I will turn around and sell them," 20-year-old Juan Campos, standing in line with his girlfriend who wants to buy a pair for her father. Ana wants to give them to her father as a Christmas present. She promised she would buy him his favorite toys when she got her first job after graduating from nursing school. Now that she had been working at a nearby hospital and earning a decent salary, she wanted to keep her promise.

Not too far from Juan and Ana, stood a couple of guys who had been smoking a rough substance in a long pipe. They passed around very often to take a few puffs. Despite the discomfort clearly expressed by some shoppers standing around them, nobody dared say anything. Those guys were loud and obnoxious. They sounded like most young Americans traveling overseas. It was as if they wanted the rest of shoppers to listen to them. They wanted an audience. They were cussing, calling others names, and making coded reference to their illicit activities without any shame and fear. That was way before voters in many states were thinking about legalizing marijuana. They talked about their stash of pot while standing in line, not even fearing they might get busted by a police officer standing and waiting in line. Such was the chaos that existed in those long lines.

Suddenly, when she could not take it any longer, a female shopper, later identified as Ana Marie Striker, slapped the guy standing behind her. Her boyfriend rushed back from the restroom to defend her.

"He touched my ass. I warned him the first time, but he would not stop."

"No, I did not touch your ass. My body may have brushed you by accident," responded the poor guy who feared a gang attack for disrespecting the young woman. Blushing, he had to quickly resort to this self-defense move. The poor-looking lad looked scared of being attacked by the crowd of female shoppers accompanied by brothers and boyfriends.

"Wait. I will tell my boyfriend. He is coming back right now. He will kick your ass. I texted him that you touched my ass. He told me to stay put. Why did you keep coming close to my backside?"

The young female was trying to create space around her for her friends who were on their way to shop. However, she would never let this guy off the hook.

"It's because somebody may have pushed me into you. I accidently bumped into you."

Without asking any questions, the heavily tattooed boyfriend arrived on the scene and placed his fat hand and bulging bicep under the poor lad's throat and lifted him up off the ground effortlessly. He then quickly slapped him a few times as if he wanted to show him he was the boss.

When he finally put him back down, the poor lad was out of breath and folded himself as if he wanted to breathe. He was out of breath. His face turned as red as a tomato recently harvested from the burned soil of California. Like a dog pulling his tail under himself, the young man was able to mouth a few crazy statements and crawled out of the line. With lots of shame and a few tears in his face, he walked away until he reached his car in the ocean of vehicles parked in the nearby parking lot. Trying to keep peace, another strong-armed muscled customer came from behind the line to confront the tattooed boyfriend who had trashed the poor lad. All hell was about to break loose!

"Hey dude, that's not a way to treat people. This poor kid was here just like any other kid. He could have been my son. You picked on the wrong kid without even asking what happened. You were not here. You only listened to your girlfriend's complaints. And you lashed out at him."

"Do you want me to give you the same treatment?" asked the tattooed boyfriend, walking towards the strong-armed, large bicep good samaritan.

It was at that very moment that his girlfriend planted herself between the two quarrelling men. The boyfriend pushed her away like a piece of paper. Yet, she got up and returned to prevent the boyfriend from being crushed by the other guy. They continued to exchange words but they did not get to any physical blows yet.

"No Bruce. Do not fight this guy," cried and commanded his girlfriend, Ana Marie, who started the whole brouhaha.

"Let's get it done right here right now. You think you can just walk all over people just like that. I will bring you to justice. A corporal punishment for your stupidity."

"Let me face this puffy guy," asked the boyfriend. Ana wrapped her arm around him. She did not want to let him go. Thanks to God, the strong-armed, large bicep good samaritan did not pull him out of her embrace.

"You're lucky. Your girlfriend is protecting you. If it was not for her protection, I would make you sweep the floor with your tongue," said the strong man who wanted to stand up for the abused little guy who left.

The boyfriend found a way to get rid of his girlfriend's embrace and came too close to the muscled guy. He punched Bruce a couple of times. He socked him very well. Bruce had no time to recover from the punches. He apparently was all talk with no creative action for self-defense. By the way, the muscled guy punched and disarmed Bruce so quickly, he was assumed to be a martial art expert who would never use his special skills if it was not to correct an injustice.

Ana Marie Strike quickly got on her cellphone. She was overheard talking to a friend of Bruce. She was asking him for reimbursements.

"Hey, skin bro, bring all the brothers. Bruce is in a big problem," she said while sobbing. "A guy just knocked him to the ground. We need all the skinheads you can find. Tell them we are at the mall. Bruce is not responding well now," she said.

"Where are you now?" asked the brother on the other line.

"We have been waiting for the store to open so we can buy the new Air Jordan."

"Ok. Wait for us there. We are coming. We're on our way. We'll castrate this mother-fucker. We'll make him pay for beating Bruce."

Ana Marie went back to Bruce who was still resting on his back. A female Emergency Responder (ER) took control of the scene. More police officers were called in by the security guards. Other customers, witnessing the melee, quickly called for police reinforcements who arrived within minutes. The mall police officers were busy in the front of the long line. They could not see what was happening towards the end of this long line or around the corner of the building on that day.

The mall police officers quickly quickly called another ambulance and secured the scene of the incident. They were ready to handcuff the strong, muscled guy when the rest of the customers intervened to defend him. They protested and explained to the officer that the whole brouhaha got started after the apparent victim beat up a poor lad who was then chased out of the line. This muscled guy was minding his own business. He just made a few comments about the inappropriateness of the victim's actions. The victim challenged him to a fight. This muscled guy was not about to start a fight until he was attacked by the victim. He got what he was after.

"What's the victim's name?" asked a police officer.

"Bruce is his name," replied his girlfriend, Ana Marie Striker.

"Ok. I have had enough of this charade. I need to hear it from this guy who is in detention," said a police officer. "We may have to take him to the station to interrogate him. Obviously, we have a victim."

"It was my self-defense. This guy was already high and was abusing everybody around here. I just wanted to have a few words with him. He would not want to talk to me without engaging into a fight first," said the muscled guy to the officer.

The two officers responding to the chaotic situation and the frenzy of the customers were soon rejoined by 6 more officers. In front of such a rowdy crowd, they pulled out their pepper spray and baton. They were bracing themselves for the eventuality of a full-blown riot. In the back of their mind, they were thinking about the LA riots, Watts riots, arsons, lootings and violence. They were thinking about the innocent bystanders. They were thinking about the worse set of events that could happen there. They were old enough to understand the psychology of crowd violence.

"Ok. I am going to handcuff you for your own good and our protection."

The muscle guy complied. Then he was led away to one of the police vehicles parked far away from the crowd.

"Tell us what happened here tonight," said one of the officers on the scene. "Cooperate with us so we can have a good night."

"I was standing behind two other customers when I witnessed this tough guy strking a young man whom his girlfriend had wrongly accused of touching her buttocks."

"Where is this young man who was victimized?" asked the officer, writing in his pad.

"He was chased out of the line by Bruce," said the muscled guy, pointing at his own victim.

"What's your name?" asked the interrogating officer.

"My name is Marshall Matters."

"Ok, Marshall Matters. How did you cause this strong, tattooed man to drop to the ground like a dried leaf?"

"All I can say is that I reacted in my self-defense. I would have never thrown the first blow. I just wanted to control an out-of-control young man who thought he could beat a kid who could be my son."

"But he is the only victim now, Mr. Matters. Would you know how he fell to the ground this way?"

"Well, he struck me in the face first. I have witnesses here who talked to another officer about what happened. I only had to defend myself and prevent him from hurting more customers who had been waiting in the cold without any problem."

"I am still not convinced about how you were able to fell such a giant. I have known him and met him in other brawls all around the city. He has a rapsheet," said the officer.

"Well, sir, if you must know, I am a black belt karate sensei. I run a karate and judo club in the valley and in the Bay area. I do not use my skills lightly. I only use them to protect, serve and defend," said Mr. Matters who competed in various international competitions. He competed agains the best in the world. He also has a degree in business.

On that fateful and cold December day, Mr. Matters was waiting in line just like any other shoppers. He was on a mission to surprise his son who was set to return from Iraq after three successful and consecutive tours of services. He was surprised of his son's service to the nation. Earlier the night before, he had received a call from his son, Victorian, about his interest in owning a pair of the sneakers. He promised he would put his neck out to try to secure a pair for him. He could have sent one of his employees, but he wanted to be part of the shopping experience. He wanted it to be meaningful for both of them. After all, he knew what it was like to return home from the war. Mr Marshalls, himself, was a Desert Storm war veteran. Victorian's grandfather, Albert Marshalls, was a vietnam veteran who had received his dues. He came back from the war filling unappreciated and vilified.

The country was not ready to welcome vietnam vets. It was not prepared to validate and appreciate his courage in that country. Such was not Mr. Marshalls' fate when he returned from

Desert Storm. His return was very different from that of Victorian's grandfather. The Matters have had a long history of serving the country. At the drop of a hat, they were willing to serve and leave to defend the nation. To go to the front lines, they would leave family, friends and business behind. They were willing to defend the freedom and rights that all Americans hold dear to their heart. On that chaotic, cold night, the memories of his years of sacrifice and service came flashing back and flooding his mind. He could not live with himself to see that his father, his son, and he have been willing to go to foreign soils to defend the freedom of complete strangers when an opportunity to defend a skinny, younger man against a bully named Bruce presented itself. He wanted to make a difference in this young man's life. He wanted to defend his honor. Mr. Marshalls was the right guy at the right place. He saw the face of his own son in this defeated and isolated young man. He wanted to redress a wrong. That is why he volunteered to have a simple talk with Bruce who had egged him on and threatened to mistreat him like his young victim.

At any moment, Mr. Marshalls would leave to welcome his son back into the country. The U.S.A. president had ended the Iraq chapter of the long war against terrorism. "Welcome back home, welcome back home, welcome back," he said the American troops that had already crossed the Iraq borders. Victorian Marshalls made it safely to a US base in a nearby friendly country en route to the USA. Mr. Marshalls remained in direct contact with his son. The two men were very close. Following in his own father's footsteps, Victorian was proud of the sacrifices had consented to while he was growing up. He had heard the stories of his grandfather's war service. Wars fought in very different theaters did one thing. They united those three men for ever.

The ambulance had already arrived on the scene. The first responders revived and treated Bruce who was left dazed by the shock of the blows to his system. In his condition, he only wanted one thing. He wanted to go back home to rest. He did not care about the sneakers any longer. Yet, his girlfriend swore to stay put so she can get her hands on a few pairs of shoes. She was also waiting for reinforcements who coud arrive any minutes. She was hoping that the police officers would leave and create enough space for her bands of skinhead bros to come down to inflict enough damage to the muscled man, Mr. Marshalls. To her surprise, one of the police officers continued to interrogate him. He had his handcuffs in his hands but he refused to Mr. Marshalls' wrist. The two men appeared to be enthralled by this long topic. Ana Marie Striker was not close to be able to overhear anything they were saying to each other.

"You are my age. I just want to know you a little bit more. In which branch of the army have you served?" asked the police officer after the two men had been conversing for more than 50 minutes. There were enough police officers on the scene to secure the rest of the mall parking lot. Yet, a yellow ribbon kept the triage area separated from the onlookers' long line.

"I am a Desert Storm veteran. I fought in the sand dunes of Saddam Hussein. We defeated him. We captured after pulling him out of a rat hole. I served two tours of service," replied Mr. Marshalls.

"Wow, that is great. You were in the front line too!"

"Yes, sir. I operated a Humvee in the front line."

"I was a heavey machine tech. These days, they call them heavy machine engineers. I did that until I got shot on my left shoulder. I have the scars to show for my service."

The two men shook hands as if they wanted to each other, "Welcome back, brother. Thanks for your service. I will get your back."

The officer bid farewell to Mr. Marshalls after exchanging phone numbers. He asked him to go near the front of the line to avoid any futher reprisals. He also talked to his buddies to keep an eye on him.

The police officer consulted with the leader of the dispatch and walked toward the area where Bruce retreated.

"Bruce, you are under arrest for disorderly conduct and destroying public peace. You and your girlfriend started the trouble tonight. Turn around. Do not put up a fight before I take your girlfriend too."

Unlike the previous arrests, Bruce did not put up a fight this time. In the past, he used to be drunk and under the influence of some hardcore drugs. This time, he was sober after being revived from his long period of blackout. Bruce blew a kiss to his girlfriend who promised to carry on and stand up for him. Ana Marie was an avid collector of Nike Air Jordan sneakers. She was not going to lose her spot in the line. She was lucky this time. The police officer did not take her to the local jail that night. She was not going to abandon her prime spot in the line.

Handcuffed behind his back, Bruce was led to a waiting police car driven by a canine police officer. That female canine was a Desert storm veteran who continued to serve the nation with this police force. Operation Second Chance was the name of the K9 held in the back of the vehicle, a spit away from Bruce. She was dispatched on several tours. She was a black german shepherd that was as elegant, smart as furious when launched after the city's underground criminals. Operation Second Chance caught so many drug dealers, gang members, pimps and Johns that the companion officers have lost count. Her bark and bite were legendary. The sight of the canine reduced and brought fleeing drug dealers to their knees while they lost their body functions.

Mr. Marshalls made it a point to salute the canine when he was introduced to her in the waiting squad car before Bruce got in reluctantly. He could not help but think about the great contributions of those specialized dogs in sniffing out IUDs and other explosive devices buried under the hot sun and sands of Iraq during the Desert Storm deployment. At that time, Victorian was a high school young man who was thrilling the local community on the football field every Friday night. Mr. Marshalls received those amazing email messages when he was near or at the base. When he was deployed deep into Iraq, it was hard for him to access a laptop to skype his family or read their email.

Operation Second Chance was also busy catching some of the former classmates of Victorian whose lives took a wrong turn. Many of them refused to work hard to earn their money. They had decided to leave the livestyle of the rich and the (in) famous. They wanted to drive the fancy hotrods. They wanted to have the well-decorated home located in the best part of the town without putting in any hard work and education. Staying in school was not their thing. They were more street-savy than anything else. They wanted all the blink and luxury their eyes had ever caught a glimpse of. They wanted to take the easy way out. They never cared about reading a book about how the rich they wanted to imitate became rich. They wanted to go down the path of least resistance. They were willing to engage in human trafficking, sex and drug trafficking just to make the money they needed. They were willing to engage in any criminal activities to earn money. They had no loyalty to nobody. They were ready to live the cut-throat lifestyle.

One of Victorian's former classmates and football friends became a major drug dealer whose notoriety for crimes gave him the honor of being wanted by the FBI. He easily made the "Most Wanted List." He had been on the run since the last time Drug Enforcement Team paid a visit to one of his residences in the hill. He was on his way back home when one of his spies gave him a tip of the ransaking of his home. Just like that, he slipped through the cracks. The FBI and local authorities had been hot on his trail/tail since that near miss. He had been rumored to form alliance with Mexican drug dealers who sheltered him in the border towns. He sought refuge from these guys after deciding to network them with his U.S. partners in crime. Mr. Marshalls gave thanks to God every day that his favorite son, Victorian, chose to join the U.S. forces and make something of his life. For one thing, he was not running around on the streets.

Less than 10 minutes after the squad car had departed, Ana Marie Striker's reinforcements arrived on the scene. A group of 15 shaved heads pretended to join the shopping line. They wanted to buy Nike Air Jordan shoes too. Those burly young men descended on the parking lot. They converged to the area where Ana Marie had described. The hatred on their face scared most parents who were still braving the cold elements of the December weather patterns and freeze. They were carrying their phones and some other items under their clothing. Four police officers who were assigned to control and watch the middle of the line rushed to intercept them. But before they arrived at that destination, the young men decided to create problems for many customers who were waiting in line. All of them forced their way to the lines, cutting in front of customers who had been waiting for hours only to find themselves being shoved back. They did not take this disrespect calmly. They called for help and denouced them quickly.

One by one, the police officers flushed them out of the lines with the assistance of the waiting consumers. They decided to threaten the customers right in the presence of the officers who pepper sprayed some of the worst troublemakers.

Ana Marie Striker came running to try to intercede in their favor. She did not know that the police officers were keeping track of her actions. They knew who she was. They knew she was allied with those troublemakers. The officers had already found out she had made some phone calls to seek reinforcements. They were ready for them and for her.

In less than 1 minute, the scene was flushed with returning backup officers who quickly placed all the skinheads under arrest in various waiting squad cars. They did not have time to throw any blows that time. For sure, they caused the shoppers and managers' nerves to be frayed a little bit.

The Nike Air Jordan Retro XI sneakers modeled after the 1996 originals were designed for Michael Jordan when he played for Chicago Bulls. They raised the right emotion in all those customers waiting in line for hours. They also responded to some specific needs and desires. Those shoes were the modification and spinning of an old successful product that was released at the right time, two days before Christmas 2011.

Were the marketing and buzz campaigns too strong? They were the marketer's jewels. Nike ended up reaping its benefits. So did Michael Jordan. The hype they created all over the country and the world connected with the mass of consumers. When diffused by social media and picked up by the regular press, they bordered insanity as shown all over the country through the riots and stampedes at the malls.

Mixing emotions with commerce tends to produce exceptional results as proven by the riots, stampedes, and pepper spray discharged on unruly shoppers all over the country all over the country and the world. Despite the current conditions of the economy, fellow American consumers are willing to shell more than $200 including tax on a pair of shoes. The hot sales of these sneakers proves that the American and world consumers will do anything to purchase the product of their desires. Whether they convey a certain status or retain their resale value on some marketplaces, pawn shops where they can be sold for twice as much, these shoes are clear staples of the shoppers' consumerism. They represent their rights to shop, self-entitlement, and happiness.

Now the question to ask is whether all of these people went out to buy the shoes to give as gifts or to be able to make some quick bucks. It would be ridiculous to think that all of them will be gifted away. They are and will remain primarily gifts to the buyers. Like gold, they will not get rid of them soon. Some collectors, running low on cash, may want to pawn some of their least popular shoes. Other collectors will not even wear them. They may take them out of their room on special occasions, especially when close and trusted friends come over. Some of these shoes are in such high demand that a few people are willing to kill over them. So they will be stored away for a long time. They will not be worn in the public or any public functions. That is mostly the domain of high quality, luxurious sneaker collectors.

Chapter 3
Nike Air Jordan Retro Sneakers, 'If I Could Be Like Mike' Advertising,
and the JORDAN Brand

Nike's marketing team must have been very proud of their efforts to place their top gear in the hands of consumers all over the country and the rest of the world. As Nike became a very bold marketer, Michael Jordan became a human marketing piece too. By then, he was and remains a walking, talking billboard that just happens to be a spokeman for Nike. His talent also sold his product. Nike was determined to market Michael Jordan. At the same time, Michael Jordan knew that he had to market himself and the products and companies he represented. He knew that he had to be a role model. He was always a well-dressed, well-mannered, good natured and respectable person. He knew he did not have to join the group of players whose body was covered with tattoos. To become a worldwide icon, he had to stay above the fray.

It was clear that at that point Nike was ready to promote the Air Jordan line and later the AIR FORCE and AIR FLIGHT lines. The commercials that aimed at glorifying Jordan and showing his humble, down-to-earth personality also sold the Air Jordan shoes. Nike was raking in the cash. Some industry insiders reported that Nike made over $4 Billion during that time. Some of the commercials showed Jordan doing things that young as well as old people would dream of doing. Jordan was soaring through the air. He gave the audience the impression he was hung from the sky. Yet, in the background, his fans could hear the chorus, "If I could be like Mike.." From the sky, Jordan would dunk the basketball. For sure, Nike was able to turn Michael Jordan into the athlete of any age group. The company started producing sizes from infant and up. In the 1990s, Nike's AIR JORDAn sneakers became the bestselling and most popular basketball shoes on the market. Nike was eclipsing its competitors, Adidas and Reebok. Actually, there was no competion.

Even after Jordan retired from basketball, his brand, The Jordan Brand, continued to be successful. It's worth noting that The Jordan Brand is a separate business unit from the Nike Brand. Jordan had long become a brand by himself. All the fans wanted to see what Jordan was wearing and doing all the times. After all, Jordan became their dream. The fans were ready to buuy the product he endorses. In so doing, the consumers felt that they could come a little closer to their hero.

Nike's retro collection brought back Jordan's past shoes which sold very well despite their high price. Nike even sold Jordan's college gear such as shoes, shirts, and shorts. While bypassing the market penetration stage, the Jordan Brand went directly to the most profitable stage. It is worth taking a look at the top athletes that side with the Jordan Brand and the Nike team.

Some of the top athletes that side with the Jordan Brand are: Bake Griffin, Kawhi Leonard, Jimmy Butler, Russel Westbrook, Chris Paul, Derek Jeter and Carmelo Anthony. The Jordan Brand continues to grow and encompass other sports and sports figures. For example, it has top Football players such as Randy Moss, Golfer Tiger Woods etc. The Jordan Brand also sponsors Penn State University, Florida State University, and his alma mater, North Carolina. At the same time, the Jordan Brand got into the well-established tradition of making shoes and apparel for the athete and by the athlete.

On the Nike Brand, we find top players such as Kobe Bryant who retired a few years ago, Lebron James, Paul Georges, Kyrie Irving, Kevin Durant. At one point, Nike endorsed Eddie Jones, Ray Allen, Michael Finley, Scottie Pippen of the Chicago Bulls, and Kevin Garnett.

At the end of the day, Michael Jordan provides the following advice:

1. Put in work
2. You must try
3. Attitude is everything.
4. Prepare to fail
5. Stay committed.

Chapter 4

The Jordan Brand: Sneakers, Athletic Footwear, Apparel, and Gear From the Renowned Chicago Bulls Basketball Player Michael Jordan

The Jordan Brand is the coronation or peak of Michael Jordan's amazing basketball career with the Chicago Bulls. While entertaining his global fan base, Michael was also interested in business. After signing up with Nike Inc., he managed to learn a little bit of the business side from the company's founders. He was one of the very bright players who would ask key questions. He realized that it was not worth playing ball only. He needed to invest in his future by building a series of businesses that will bring him money after his retirement. Michael started understanding the various types of markets that exist. He had to learn about the Law of Demand, Supply and Demand and many important business fundamentals from the school of hard knocks. He had to return to the textbooks, the business books.

'There are broad markets, thin markets,
Stable markets, big ones
There are fish markets, flea markets
Gem markets, money markets
Fruit markets, gold markets
Free markets, dope markets
Controlled markets, sloppy ones
Meat markets, luxury markets
Indeed there are lots of markets in this world.'

Michael Jordan needed to launch his business to be successful. He wanted to play a different kind of games. He was in it to win. After all, to be successful in business, he needed to have good information about all the aspects of his operation. He knew he did not have to go through the market penetration stage. The 6 championships he won for the Chicago Bulls already gave him not only name recognition but also quality of any products he would endorse or produce. He knew he had already cornered a large group of his fans in the footwear and apparel markets. So from his early days with Nike and thanks to the Nike marketing staff, he started focusing on these key determinants of demand: Tastes and preferences, targeting buyers' incomes so they can buy the sneakers via demographics and psychographics (Analytics), Number of people or competitors in the market of footwear, expectations or the demand for the shoes, and advertisement. In Michael Jordan's case, he became a walking, talking marketer and had global name recognition. All he needed to do was spin his celebrity earned on the basketball court to the business world. Up to this point, he knew that he could turn his fans into avid buyers of his products. He promised to deliver them top brand, quality merchandise, and affordable price on limited supply. Thanks to the law of supply, Nike marketers realized that it was time to bring back Michael Jordan's University of North Carolina clothes and old Bulls wear. They named it Nike Air Jordan Retro. Consumers were in line to buy a few pairs. When the price of the shoes went up, so did Nike's profits. Various industry insiders stated that Nike made $billions in the 1980s with this marketing campaign.

So from the crib to the coffin, The Jordan Brand has some athletic footwear and apparel for the brand-savvy consumers. In fact, it's been said that kids are a 'dream target' to most marketers. Nike and Michael Jordan knew how teenagers can influence their parents' buying power. At the end of the shopping experience, parents often crack and complete the sale. More and more kids are spending more than pennies. They know what they want. So they may have been saving for this specific brand. Therefore, they own a high degree of knowledge about products and brands. In school, they learn from their friends. They do not want to be victimized by those who attribute positive and negative characteristics to others depending on their product usage. A parent once said, "When you are a kid, it's not what you drive, it's what you carry (wear) that gives you status in the blackboard jungle. And nowadays when all kids spot a cellphone, social media become the new make or break tools used by many of them..'

Wearing a pair of Jordan sneakers instead of a pair of Converse helps kids make friends easily. The youth sophisticates know exactly what to wear. They sometimes force their parents to buy exactly what they want. For example, both boys and girls, aged 9 to 12 are regular users of deodorant, perfume, fragrance, eau de cologne, and nail polish. All of them tend to use hair mousse.

Why do marketers get interested in kids? Why does Michael Jordan produce athletic shoes and apparel for kids? If Nike does not focus on this growing market, then its competitors will embrace them.

Marketers are interested in kids who buy their brand now because they will most likely remain interested in them later. Nike and The Jordan Brand are forward-looking companies that realize that brand loyalties form at an early age. This way, they will have time to cement those bonds with their future products. It's worth taking a look at how the McDonald's Corporation sees children. In fact, McDonald's was the pioneer of the concept of preparing kids for future markets. It appeals to kids by offering meal kids, parties, playgrounds etc. That's the first phase. Then in the second phase, they realize the kids' role as influencers in the family decision making. Its advertising focuses on family trips to the restaurant.

The 3rd phase, McDonald's regards children as their future markets. This way, the Golden Arches will always consumers because kids will become parents who will bring their own kids.

The Jordan Brand borrows a few pages from McDonald's. One of them is the growing future market. Other companies do the same thing.

The shopping experience becomes a cycle. The Jordan Brand creates instant status. The buyers of the footwear feel they are part of a special group. They share common interests. Just like owners of motorcycle can form a club, Jordan collectors exist too from China, Japan to the US and Europe. The social experiences and interpersonal attraction are sometimes the main motives. The thrill of the chase can be observed in the parking lot where buyers wait in line for hours. They want to shop till they drop. They were born to shop. 'When the going gets tough, the tough go shopping.' Now, one can understand why the malls of this country are filled with young men and women who are walking up and down. They visit the shoe stores to mingle and share their footwear experience.

Over the years, superstar Michael Jordan has become a sacred hero. He was thought to have superhuman powers. Otherwise, he would not throw the winning baskets leading to the Bulls championship. Fans will argue for hours some of his championship games. Michael proved he was one when others thought he could not win the championship game. Yet, he managed to deliver the winning basket under strenuous circumstances.

Even though Michael Jordan retired from basketball, his fans continue to watch his games on YouTube. The lifestyle he promotes continues to attract new fans who become new buyers of his products. It makes sense to buy a basketball team to stay in the game. It was a great business decision. All it takes is for fans to take a look at the Jordan Brand list of sponsored ballers who are NBA standouts such as Russell Westbrook of Oklahoma City Thunder, Carmelo Anthony New York Nicks, Jimmy Butler of the Chicago Bulls etc.

Nowadays, shoppers may not need to go wait in line to buy a pair of Nike or Jordan shoes. From their smartphones or other devices, they can make a purchase with a few clicks. They can sign up to receive updates. They can click on a link on the various social media sites to shop online. From Twitter, Facebook, Instagram etc, they can shop in the comfort of their home any time. Technology makes shopping easier these days.

Past Advertising Notes:

1. Road jam, cloud jam, space jam, and mall jam for Nike Air Jordan XI Concord Sneakers: An updated version of the fictionalized Success Story – Michael Jordan as a live billboard
2. The new sub-culture of sneaker collectors and the Rise of Sneaker Nation
3. Updates on the story of the Jordan Brand and Nike Sneakers – An urban fiction/nonfiction. An urban thriller. 2011-2017 edition
4. Word of mouth, word on the Main streets, and buzz marketing principles
5. Overview / diffused sneak peek: Hail to the King of Sneakers
6. A few pairs of the most popular Nike Air Jordan Sneakers. Some of them caused frenzy, chaos, and the stabbing of a shopper at Newport Center in New Jersey back in 2011.

eBook Review:

"Hail to the King of Sneakers: Michael Jordan's Nike Air Jordan Retro Time (A Social Media-loaded Marketing Campaign Success Story)" is an ebook about the history of Michael Jordan's superhero, superstar basketball player who ended up becoming a great businessman after his retirement. It's also the story of sneaker collectors who did not mind staying in line to be able to buy a few pairs of his shoes. Over the years, superstar Michael Jordan has become a sacred hero. He was thought to have superhuman powers. In this ebook, you will read about the shopping incidents, Michael's business advice, and hard-working skills. You will also read about the shoe empire he ends up building and the standout players who are part of his brand.

Michael Jordan produces shoes for his fans and consumers of all age group. In his mind, kids are his future markets. Find out where he got started and what he had to do to build this luxury shoe empire. From the school of hard knocks to various business textbooks and the key questions he had to ask, you will find out he was a determined player and businessman who wants to make a difference in this world.

References: Special Notes

1. Nike Air Jordan, Nike Air Jordan XI Concord, and the shoes above are either trademarks, brands, or special product editions of Nike Inc. The photos used in this work of reality-based fiction belong to the company. They are only used here for illustration purposes only. They are not for sale. As fans and shoppers, some of these pairs belong to each one of us. As a corporation, Nike promotes safety and security in the sale of its products.

1. Michael Jordan played for the Chicago Bulls until his retirement. He is a well-respected businessman who is the owner of a car company, basketball team, Charlotte Hornets, The Jordan Brand etc. His trademark moves and products are often well received by the mass of shoppers. To stay above the fray of political issues, he once said, "Republicans as well as democrats wear shoes."

Authors:

Prepared and written by Kevin Levin and Charles Desmangles, Emeritus professors of World History, Marketing, and Social Media at eCaribbean People's University.

Mr. Joseph Charles also contributed to the fictionalization of the story. He is a language expert and business consultant who provides his consulting and linguistic services to major US and international corporations vying for the global market. Contact him at Teach2Coach[at]Gmail dot com.

www.ingramcontent.com/pod-product-compliance
Lightning Source LLC
Chambersburg PA
CBHW070928220526
45468CB00005B/1698